To

M rs. Sebast ian

From

I ♥ U   Alex
         Bair

ANGELS

HEAVENLY BLESSINGS

Publications International, Ltd.

Louis Weber, C.E.O.
Publications International, Ltd.
7373 North Cicero Avenue
Lincolnwood, Illinois 60646

Permission is never granted for commercial purposes.

Manufactured in China.

8 7 6 5 4 3 2 1

ISBN: 0-7853-2821-1

The inspirations in this book were written and compiled by Carol Smith, who earned a master's degree in religious education from Southwestern Seminary in Fort Worth, Texas. She has worked as a children's minister and freelance writer, contributing to a wide variety of publications and magazines, including *Bible Dictionary for Kids* and *The Treasure Bible*.

Acknowlegements:
Publications International, Ltd., has made every effort to locate the owners of all copyrighted material to obtain permission to use the selections that appear in this book. Any errors or omissions are unintentional; corrections, if necessary, will be made in future editions.

Pages 26–27: Taken from *A Rustle of Angels* by Marilyn Carlson Webber and William D. Webber. Copyright © 1994 by Marilyn Carlson Webber and William D. Webber. Used by permission of Zondervan Publishing House.

Page 31: Taken from *A Book Of Angels* by Sophy Burnham, Copyright © 1990 by Sophy Burnham. Reprinted by permission of Ballantine Books, a Division of Random House, Inc.

Page 53: Taken from *A Book Of Angels* by Sophy Burnham, Copyright © 1990 by Sophy Burnham. Reprinted by permission of Ballantine Books, a Division of Random House, Inc.

CONTENTS

ANGELS ABOVE US

Since ancient times,
angels have carried messages
from Heaven to Earth—
messages of joy, of pain,
of children, and of nations.

ANGELS ABOVE US

Angels are a society.
They are a civilization.
They are a life-form, a culture.
They are created like we are,
but with a different purpose and
in a different realm.
They have tasks they perform,
and they watch humans
with interest.
They interact in our lives and guide
our journey through life.

ANGELS ABOVE US

No matter how alone you feel,
when you look to the left and
look to the right, you'll find your
journey is a shared one.

ANGELS ABOVE US

ANGELS

Angels have always been with us,
in every time and culture. Ever since we
emerged from the dim, distant past there
have been records and representations of
another race of beings who share this
world with us. In pictograms and
paintings, poetry and children's stories,
our ancestors down through the ages have
tried to pass on what they knew about
these beings. In the last few hundred years
we have come to believe that something
is real only if we can see it through
a microscope or telescope. But no
telescope will ever be powerful enough
to see into the angelic realms.
This doesn't faze the angels one bit.

ALMA DANIEL

ANGELS ABOVE US

ANGELS ABOVE US

ANGELS ABOVE US

ANGELS

When I think of an angel,
I think of a floating, celestial being.
I think of an angel as someone who has
only good thoughts, never bad.
I see them always with a glow and always
pleasant and completely centered.
I picture them with such a
sense of purpose,
so connected to their reason for being,
that they never lose their way.
I see angels as the kind of being
I would like to be.

ANGELS ABOVE US

I'd like to see an angel dance.
I'd like to dance along.

ANGELS ABOVE US

ANGELS

The more we become like angels,
the more we give great gifts to the world.
And the more we feel unity with
every bird,
every rock and wild flower,
every inch of atmosphere and
drop of water,
the more alive we are.
The more we see and know ourselves
everywhere in all people,
in all things,
the more we admit the presence
of Glory in our own humble,
sacred hearts.

KAREN GOLDMAN

ANGELS ABOVE US

17

A halo, you know,
is not some ring around
an angel's head.
It is a glow,
an aura that surrounds
their physical image.
It is a light that has no globe,
a moonlit sky without a moon.
It is an attempt to capture
our attention so we'll listen for an
important message.

ANGELS ABOVE US

Angels are the unseen hands
that applaud you and
the heavenly voices that
cheer you on.
All you have to do is listen
and look with your heart.

ANGELS ABOVE US

ANGELS WHO GUARD US AND GUIDE US

See, I am sending an angel
ahead of you to guard you
along the way and to bring you
to the place I have prepared.

EXODUS 23:20

ANGELS

ANGELS WHO GUARD US AND GUIDE US

It is said—and it is true—
that just before we are born,
a cavern angel holds his finger to our
mouths and whispers,
"Hush! Don't tell what you know."
This is why we have a cleft on our
upper lips and remember nothing of
where we came from.

RODERICK MacLEISH

Are not all angels ministering
spirits sent to serve those who
will inherit salvation?

HEBREWS 1:14

ANGELS WHO GUARD US AND GUIDE US

23

Halos and wings and harps and strings.
Is that an angel's world? Are their streets
made of gold, adorned with clockless
cathedrals, surrounding a celestial park?
Not for guardian angels. These are the
beings spanning the beauty of Heaven
and the sometimes harsh reality of Earth.
They are the ones sweeping through the
city at the speed of humans, following,
with care, their charges full of
stubborn will and free spirit. They are
the ones standing watch over lives
undaunted. And whether or not
we acknowledge their presence,
they remain by our side—always.

ANGELS WHO GUARD US AND GUIDE US

ANGELS

ANGELS WHO GUARD US AND GUIDE US

Sam Johnston tells of when his father had
a job transfer from one area of the
country to another. The family managed
to pack everything they owned into a
trailer, which they bolted to their car.

Sam's mother took the first driving shift.
She drove faster than she should have
and was stopped by an officer,
who pulled her over and gave her a kind
warning to slow down.

Sam's parents traded places while they
were pulled over. Perhaps a minute after
their start-up, a tire came off the car!
The car was still going slowly enough
for Sam's dad to be able to bring the
car and trailer to a safe stop.

All of them sat stunned, only guessing
what would have happened if they had
been still going seventy miles per hour.
The family immediately looked back
to thank the officer—but he was gone.
He wasn't on the road behind them,
and there was no way he could have
crossed the median.
He had simply disappeared.

MARILYNN CARLSON WEBBER

ANGELS WHO GUARD US AND GUIDE US

My father, when he was a small boy,
was climbing on an upper story of a
house that was being built.
He walked to the end of a board
that was not nailed at the other end,
and it slowly began to tip.
He knew that he was doomed,
but inexplicably the board began
to tip the other way,
as though a hand had pushed
it down again.
He always wondered whether it
was an angel's hand.

ELISABETH ELLIOT

ANGELS WHO GUARD US AND GUIDE US

Thank you, angels,
for seeing me through.
Thanks for all the caring
things you do.
Thanks for being aware,
through times of struggle and despair,
for being so faithful,
so I can feel more carefree
just knowing you are there.

ANGELS WHO GUARD US AND GUIDE US

Somewhere on this long and winding
road of life you will need to be rescued,
whether you realize it or not.
Every night, as you close your eyes
and prepare for another night's
peaceful bliss, be grateful;
just in case today was that day.

ANGELS WHO GUARD US AND GUIDE US

A shiver runs down your spine
when you realize it is not
our imagination.
Something is watching us out there.

SOPHY BURNHAM

ANGELS WHO GUARD US AND GUIDE US

ANGELS ALL AROUND

In the flowers that I smell and the
music that I hear,
In the rain upon the window and in
the salt of every tear,
In the gentlest of moments and the
simplest of times,
I can find a hidden angel and
imagine that she's mine.

ANGELS ALL AROUND

They flutter, they flicker,
they flash, and they fly.
They skim along, soar above,
sail through the sky.
They dart and they dance,
they dash all around.
They hover and sweep,
not making a sound.
They plunge and they launch,
they sail like a breeze.

ANGELS ALL AROUND

They worship and tremble and
fall on their knees.
They rescue, they liberate,
guard, and preserve.
They give us protection,
they give us the nerve
To stand a bit taller,
to trust a bit more,
To face disappointment,
both feet on the floor,
To revere and hope in a place
they call home,
To live with the knowledge
we're never alone.

ANGELS ALL AROUND

Angels skip along the
seashore picking up shells, kissing each
one, and whisper, "Good job!"

Angels traipse through the galaxy,
touching stars and dancing on planets.

Angels waltz through the heavens,
full of joy and worship,
flowing with majesty, rhythm, and love.

ANGELS ALL AROUND

ANGELS

Every time I pass a playground
full of children,
I see the faces of angels laughing
and playing.

ANGELS ALL AROUND

ANGELS

The angels in my life are often
very familiar in form.
When I was sick,
I thought an angel touched my
forehead with a cool cloth,
but it was my mom.
When I was afraid,
I thought an angel comforted me,
but it was my brother.
When I was alone,
I thought an angel sat beside me,
but it was my friend.
Looking back now,
I wonder if I wasn't right the first time.

ANGELS ALL AROUND

Why are we surprised that we
are not alone?
Sound waves swim around our heads
each moment,
but until we tune them in,
we never hear the message.
In the same way,
angels swarm our lives every day,
but unless we remember
how to listen,
we are never aware of
their presence.

ANGELS ALL AROUND

When an angel smiles,
the sun shines through the rain.
When an angel smiles,
the cool wind begins to blow.
When an angel smiles,
a small child wakes.
When an angel smiles,
a new flake forms of snow.
When an angel smiles,
the first autumn leaf falls.
When an angel smiles,
a musician writes a song.
When an angel smiles,
a young bird learns to call.
When an angel smiles,
somebody smiles along.

ANGELS ALL AROUND

ANGELS ALL AROUND.

Claire saw an angel dancing in the sunlight. She called her "Ginger" and danced along. No one else ever saw Ginger, but eventually they paid some high prices at the box office to see Claire dance. When the reporters asked Claire where she learned how to dance, they recognized the names of teachers and academies. But she always ended her reply by saying, "But my very first teacher was an old and dear friend."

ANGELS ALL AROUND

Old Granny Roberts who lived on
Woodgreen Lane always used to say,
"Angels bless you, my child."
We thought that odd when we were kids
walking home from school past her home.
One day we stopped to help her get her
new kitten down from the third branch
of her mimosa tree, and she said,
"Angels bless you, my children. For if they
can protect you from the bad, they can
surely guide you toward the good."

ANGELS ALL AROUND

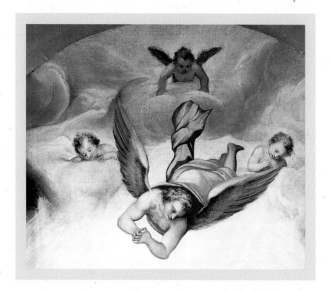

An angel reached out
and took my finger today
and squeezed it just as tight as
a baby can squeeze.

ANGELS ALL AROUND

An angel smiled at me
from her wheelchair as I passed her
window this morning.

An angel helped me into
the front door of my office
without getting wet.

You may call them a baby, a senior
citizen, or a good Samaritan,
but I say they are the angels
that follow and watch out for me
every day, making my life
more comfortable
and my awareness more real.

ANGELS ALL AROUND

ANGELS

In a world that feels powerless and alone,
I'm glad angels don't depend on our
strength to make a difference.

In a realm that sees only
the surface of things,
I'm glad angels don't depend on
our vision to make their way.

In an existence that thinks of itself
as artificial and wholly mortal,
I'm glad angels don't depend
on our belief to exist.

ANGELS ALL AROUND.

Do not forget to entertain strangers,
for by so doing some people
have entertained angels
without knowing it.

HEBREWS 13:2

ANGELS ALL AROUND

ANGEL ENCOUNTERS

But the angel said to them,
"Do not be afraid.
I bring you good news of great joy
that will be for all the people."

LUKE 2:10

ANGEL ENCOUNTERS

An angel came to me once in the form
of a black labrador puppy. My husband
and I had gone through a difficult time as
of late, and we needed some joy.
In came Wendy, a bouncing ball of fresh

ANGEL ENCOUNTERS

perspective and endless delight.
She was a little angel who reminded us
that life is bigger than our problems;
a little angel who kissed away our defenses
and played away our uneasiness;
a little angel who grew to be 60 pounds
and grew our hearts right along with her.
You may call her a pet—I'll understand
what you mean. Sometimes, though,
I catch a glimpse of her out of the
corner of my eye and I think she's tucking
in her wings so we won't know.
I think she's trying to keep us from
realizing that she was sent to us to save us
from our own complacency.
If so, she has done well.

ANGEL ENCOUNTERS

ANGELS

ANGEL ENCOUNTERS

The summer that I turned six
we had a Fresh Air child come live
with us for two weeks. It was one night
when me and Shonta were sleeping. I
woke up and saw two angels standing
in front of my closet. I didn't really feel
scared but of what I remember they didn't
have wings, like what we think of angels.
They were two men, tall men, and they
were talking softly. I will always
remember that beautiful night.

VICKI ISRAEL
SOMERSET, NEW JERSEY

ANGEL ENCOUNTERS

I thought my first grade teacher
was an angel.
She taught me how to read and write
and opened up the world to me.

I thought my second grade teacher
was an angel.
She taught me how to add and subtract
and even multiply a little.

ANGEL ENCOUNTERS

I thought my third grade teacher
was an angel.
She taught me how to write in cursive
and divide really large numbers.

I thought my fourth grade teacher
was an angel.
She gave me straight "A"s and let me
discover mystery novels.

But they were not angels, I was told.
They were just underpaid,
underappreciated people who spent their
careers helping me learn the basics of life.
I simply replied, what do you think
an angel is anyway?

ANGEL ENCOUNTERS

What do you call an angel with
a broken wing?
—an angel on the mend.

What do you call an angel with
a broken harp?
—an a cappella angel.

What do you call an angel with
a broken halo?
—an angel with a headache.

What do you call an angel with
a broken heart?
—a person who needs you.

ANGEL ENCOUNTERS

Guard me,
guide me, angels,
hide me from the troubles
all around.
Keep me safe and
give me faith to hear your steps
in every sound.

A NIGHTTIME PRAYER

ANGEL ENCOUNTERS

Where was my angel today
when my purse turned upside down
in the elevator and there wasn't even room
to pick up my stuff?

I was trying to keep the elevators clear
so that you could get to your
appointment on time.

Where was my angel today
when I was late for lunch with my boss?

I was trying to help calm you down.

ANGEL ENCOUNTERS

Where was my angel today
when I got home late from work,
ran my hose, and burned the dinner?

*I was right where I always am,
trying to help you make the best of this
tangled knot you call your life.*

ANGEL ENCOUNTERS

ANGELS

ANGEL ENCOUNTERS

I knew an angel once named Kate.
She'd spent much energy on Earth,
guarding and guiding and hoping.
She loved her charges, and had they
known her then, they would have loved
her as well. She has a different role now,
which doesn't take her as far from home,
but she loves talking about "her people."
She's so thrilled when one stops by.
She is always so amazed to discover
that they had always believed she was
there, even though they would never
have admitted it to themselves.

Sometimes in the hazy morning
between "waking up" and "not yet,"
take the time to listen to
your own soul. You'll find you
can hear your angels telling you
to be ready for the day.
It's the best wake-up call there is.

ANGEL ENCOUNTERS

When you've given all you can,
angels are watching.

When you've returned kindness
for difficulty,
angels are standing.

When you've forgiven the
unforgivable,
angels are applauding.

When you've suffered,
but not lost yourself,
angels are weeping with joy.

ANGEL ENCOUNTERS

ANGELS ARE WATCHING

Do they sit and watch us,
these angels of which we are unaware?
Do they lie on a cloud,
heads on their hands,
and peek at our world?
I think I can see them sometimes if
I look up and squint really hard.
I think I can hear them sometimes;
celestial murmurs that
accompany our hardships and will
one day lead us home.

ANGELS ARE WATCHING

We cannot help but think,
as we watch the Earth from a distance,
that you humans are both wonderful
and confusing.
You bear the image of the creator,
yet you are never happy with
the way you look.

ANGELS ARE WATCHING

You hold the hope of eternity,
yet you're always wishing for more time.
You have the capacity for
laughter and love,
yet you never feel like you have
enough of either.
You raise your offspring to be strong
and independent,
then cry to see them go.
You try to do so much on your own,
yet you could do so much more together.
You give of what you have,
yet are often afraid to give of yourself.
You keep angels busy for a lifetime,
just watching you,
but you can go a lifetime without ever
watching us back.

ANGELS ARE WATCHING

ANGELS

You may think we are shaped like tall,
gallant creatures with willowy wings
and neon halos that emanate
a heavenly glow, which is why you have
such a hard time finding us in your life.
We are sometimes a flash,
sometimes a glimpse from the corner
of your eye, but we never wear anything
neon. We often move in ways
you do not understand,
through dimensions and walls that
require neither wings nor mist.
It is a credit to your substance that you
choose not to imagine a life

ANGELS ARE WATCHING

bigger and so unlike you.
But we are.
Yet we share your world and
honor your life.
And we always will.

ANGELS ARE WATCHING

ANGELS ARE WATCHING

We never tire of telling you that
you are not alone.
We never tire of reminding you that
you are loved and valued.
We never tire of affirming your life
and your gifts.
We just always wish you knew better
how to do it for yourself as well.

ANGELS ARE WATCHING

I've been watching you, you know.
I've had my eye on you for quite some
time. It's actually my job.
When you saw that old man today in
town, the one who reminded you so much
of your granddad,
I was thinking the same thing, too.
When your feelings got hurt last night and
you didn't want anybody to know, I knew.
Always remember, through good times
and bad, I'm your angel and
you're my charge.
I will always be with you,
lighting your way, as we walk together
along life's path.

ANGELS ARE WATCHING

Angels follow our steps
as clearly as if we were
forever walking
in newly fallen snow.

ANGELS ARE WATCHING

Whenever we enter the
realm of angels,
revelations enter the heart,
bursting wide its creaky doors,
causing mountains of strength to
rise where there were none;
filling the mind with visions of
splendor and bliss that make
"reality" take a backseat to joy;
vanquishing the ordinary,
exuding the miraculous.

KAREN GOLDMAN

ANGELS ARE WATCHING

As you start each new day,
say to yourself,
"Each step of my way there is
a protector by my side,
holding my hand like
a childhood friend."

ANGELS ARE WATCHING

Photo credits

Front cover: **Planet Art**

FPG International: Jean P. De La Forest: 69; Steven Gottlieb: 39; Peter Johansky: 56; Elizabeth Simpson: 19; **Image Club:** 8, 20, 28, 31, 34, 47, 48, 54; **International Stock:** Andre Jenny: 36; Zeva Oelbaum: 29; **Planet Art:** 32; 64, 73; **SuperStock:** 50, 60; Christie's Images: 13, 37, 52, 66; Civic Museum, Padua/Mauro Magliani: 49; Cummer Museum of Art and Gardens, Jacksonville: 70; David David Gallery, Philadelphia: 30, 44, 62; Silvio Fiore: 65; Galleria Borghese, Rome/Canali PhotoBank, Milan: 11; Huntington Library Art Collections and Botanical Gardens, San Marino: 21; Library of Congress, Washington D.C.: 14; Roy Miles Gallery, London/Bridgeman Art Library, London: 25; Musee du Louvre, Paris/A.K.G., Berlin: 16; Palazzo Ducale, Mantua: 41; Private Collection/Van Hoorick Fine Art: 33; Stock Montage: 9, 23, 59; Vatican Museums & Galleries, Rome: title page, 77.

Additional photography by **Brian Warling**